D1459159

USING ARMY RECORDS

*Public Record Office*
***Pocket Guides to Family History***

Getting Started in Family History

Using Birth, Marriage and Death Records

Using Census Returns

Using Wills

Using Army Records

Using Navy Records

# USING ARMY RECORDS

PUBLIC RECORD OFFICE

Public Record Office
Richmond
Surrey
TW9 4DU

ISBN 1 873162 91 X

A catalogue card for this book
is available from the British Library

Front cover: Private G. Halsall, 4th Hussars, 25 February 1902
(PRO COPY 1/454)

Printed by Cromwell Press Ltd, Trowbridge, Wilts.

# CONTENTS

# INTRODUCTION

If you have picked up this Pocket Guide it is likely that you have already found out a great deal about your family tree. Perhaps in the course of your research you have come across an ancestor whose occupation, in a census return or on a civil registration certificate, was given as 'soldier'. Or perhaps there are indications amongst the family papers or reminiscences that an ancestor was in the Army.

There is a great wealth of records available for searching about the military aspects of your ancestors' lives, and through them it is possible to trace more detail than is available for any other profession. This Pocket Guide introduces the main types of records that are available, explains where to begin searching, and indicates avenues for further investigation. There is space only for a brief outline of the Army and its history, enough to put your initial searches in context. Some basic facts about the Army are given below as a starting point for your research.

# ORGANISATION OF THE ARMY

Before there was a standing army, the monarch would authorise members of the nobility to raise groups of men whenever soldiers were needed. These groups were called regiments, and this is still the name for the basic organisational unit of the Army, though the number of men in a regiment has varied over time. During much of their history regiments have been associated with specific areas of the country, though this has not consistently been the case. They were divided according to the following types:

- cavalry
- infantry
- artillery
- engineers

Their names were also usually defined by their military purpose, the 'light infantry' regiments, for instance, being for fast moving (and therefore lightly loaded) foot soldiers.

Regiments were often divided into two or more battalions, and this became the established practice in Victorian times, with one group of men on active service being constantly refreshed from the other battalion at home. More battalions were created in wartime when more men were needed on active duty.

Each battalion was composed of smaller groups of men (usually about a hundred) called companies in the infantry, squadrons in the cavalry and batteries in the artillery. They were divided into smaller groups again called platoons in the infantry and sections in the cavalry and artillery.

In major wars deploying huge numbers of troops, an even broader structure was employed. The total available manpower was divided into separate armies, which were each further subdivided into corps, divisions and brigades. In these armies each regiment was part of a brigade.

## Organisation chart of the Army

| Army |
| --- |
| Corps |
| Division |
| Brigade |
| Regiment |
| Company |
| Platoon |
| Section |

## Ranks

When an ordinary soldier enlisted in the Army he had to serve for a minimum of 21 years until 1871, when a period of 'short service' was introduced covering just 12 years. A private who joined the Army could be promoted through the ranks on merit (especially in time of war), in which case he was known as a non-commissioned officer. The more usual way to become an officer was to buy a commission, which was a royal warrant of appointment to a specific rank. Commissions could be bought and sold for a set price that was high enough to ensure that officers were recruited only from the wealthier ranks of society. This inegalitarian system was abolished in 1871.

The system of ranks and the names given to them evolved to meet the developing requirements of the Army. A simplified version of the most commonly held ranks is given below.

| *Commissioned officers* | *Non-commissioned officers and other ranks* |
|---|---|
| Field Marshal | Warrant Officer 1st Class |
| General | Warrant Officer 2nd Class |
| Lieutenant General | Sergeant Major |
| Major General | Staff Sergeant |
| Brigadier | Sergeant |
| Colonel | Corporal |
| Lieutenant Colonel | Lance Corporal |
| Major | Private |
| Captain | |
| Lieutenant | |
| 2nd Lieutenant | |

# SETTING OUT ON YOUR SEARCH

The basic facts that you would ideally know before you set out to trace your ancestor in the Army are:

- full name
- regiment
- rank
- number
- dates of service

If you are lucky enough to know all or most of these facts you should very soon be able to trace your ancestor's career through the mass of records available. If you know all the above details for an ancestor who was in the Second World War you can write to the Ministry of Defence (address below) for his or her service record. At present the First World War records are in the process of being transferred from the Ministry of Defence to the Public Record Office so you need to check how far this process has gone before you write for a First World War army record (see pp. 54–5). Only the next of kin can obtain a record and a fee is charged (£25 at the time of going to press).

▼ Ministry of Defence
  Army Records Centre
  Bourne Avenue
  Hayes
  Middlesex UB3 1RF

# Research at home

If you know none of the basic facts listed above, your first step is to try to discover which regiment your ancestor served in. Most army records are arranged by regiment in the archives, so the sooner you can find it out the easier your search will be. You might well find the best clues for this at home.

## *Tips for finding your ancestor's regiment*

- Any official document from the Army is likely to note a soldier's regiment.

- Medals have the regiment inscribed on them.

- Uniforms can be looked up in reference books.

- If you know the county where your ancestor lived, you could check the regiments associated with that area.

- Sometimes names of regiments appear on civil registration certificates or in census returns.

- If you know where your ancestor was living after discharge you can check the pension records, which are arranged by the districts in which the pensions were paid.

Military memorabilia are among the records most likely to have survived in the family. One reason for this is the sheer number and variety of them. The Army had to keep careful records of every aspect of each soldier's life, and therefore each soldier did too. Personal service records included not only details of postings, promotions and other army business, but also a record of appearance, kept for identification purposes in case of desertion or death. There were records of skills attained, illness and disability and eventually of discharge and pension. Any of these documents issued to a soldier by the Army is likely to list his regiment, rank and number.

Much can be learnt from other memorabilia. Medals have very often been kept in the family in remembrance of bravery and battles fought. All medals should have name, rank, number and regiment inscribed on them. Photographs are another useful source of information. It was customary for soldiers to have their photographs taken in full uniform at the beginning of active service, and these were sent home and treasured by the family. You can use old photographs to identify a uniform, a button or a badge in one of the many identification books available. A selection of these is listed in the Further Reading section.

---

### ⓘ Remember

If you have a picture of an ancestor in uniform, take it to the reference library. There are many books available to help you identify the regiment.

---

Perhaps you have only a battle reminiscence to go on, or a clue that your ancestor was posted to a foreign location. The family porcelain might come unexpectedly from Hong Kong or you might have a collection of Indian ivory. A marriage certificate might indicate a foreign origin of a wife. How did your ancestor meet her? Or a child might have been born abroad. It takes ingenuity to find a name and regiment from such scant information, but it is often possible, and there are many resources to help you. There are many places where you can research military history and the whereabouts of particular regiments at particular times. Two of the most comprehensive reference resources are:

▼ Imperial War Museum
   Department of Documents
   Lambeth Road
   London SE1 6HZ
   Telephone: 020 7416 5221

▼ National Army Museum
   Department of Records Royal
   Hospital Road
   London SW3 4HT
   Telephone: 020 7730 0717

Remember, though, that neither of these has amassed personal records for searching, so that unless your ancestor was famous or particularly heroic you will be lucky to find him individually mentioned in the regimental and general army archives and libraries.

When you have found out as much as possible about a relative who was in the Army, you need to determine, out of the great wealth of army records, which are the ones to search. This depends on a number of factors but the most important are:

- rank
- period of service

You need to plan your search carefully and keep a written note of its progress so that you do not accidentally find yourself repeating a line of enquiry. Knowing a campaign or battle in which your ancestor fought can provide a fruitful starting point.

## WHERE TO GO TO SEARCH FOR ARMY RECORDS

The full range of records of people serving in the Army is beyond the scope of this Pocket Guide, which is aimed at setting you off on the right track. For a more comprehensive list see, for example, Fowler and Spencer, *Army Records for Family Historians* or the PRO's *Alphabetical Guide*.

# Public Record Office (PRO)

The best place to start your research for any army service before 1923 is the Public Record Office. At its main site in Kew the PRO holds the official War Office records, 1660–1964. There is also an extensive library on military history and many reference books and finding aids. At the Family Records Centre (FRC) in central London, access is available to indexes of deaths in the First and Second World Wars and to regimental registers of births, marriages and deaths.

▼ Public Record Office
Kew
Richmond
Surrey TW9 4DU
General telephone: 020 8876 3444
Telephone number for enquiries: 020 8392 5200
Telephone number for advance ordering of documents (with exact references only): 020 8392 5260
Internet: http://www.pro.gov.uk/


Opening times (closed Sundays and Bank Holidays)

| Monday | 9.00 a.m. to 5 p.m. |
|---|---|
| Tuesday | 10 a.m. to 7 p.m. |
| Wednesday | 9.00 a.m. to 5 p.m. |
| Thursday | 9.00 a.m. to 7 p.m. |
| Friday | 9.00 a.m. to 5 p.m. |
| Saturday | 9.30 a.m. to 5 p.m. |

No appointment is needed to visit the PRO in Kew, though you may have to order some of the documents you require for your research in advance. You will need a reader's ticket to gain access to the research areas. To obtain a ticket you need to take with you a full UK driving licence or a UK banker's card or a passport if you are a British citizen, and your passport or national identity card if you are not a British citizen. Note that the last time for ordering documents is 4 p.m. on Mondays, Wednesdays and

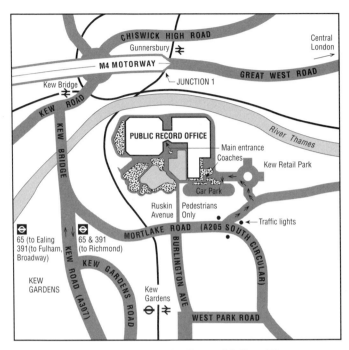

How to find the Public Record Office, Kew

Fridays; 4.30 p.m. on Tuesdays and Thursdays, and 2.30
p.m. on Saturdays.

▼ Family Records Centre
   1 Myddelton Street
   London EC1R 1UW
   General telephone: 020 8392 5300
   Fax: 020 8392 5307
   Internet: http://www.pro.gov.uk/

   Opening times (closed Sundays and Bank Holidays)

   | Monday    | 9 a.m. to 5 p.m.    |
   |-----------|---------------------|
   | Tuesday   | 10 a.m. to 7 p.m.   |
   | Wednesday | 9 a.m. to 5 p.m.    |
   | Thursday  | 9 a.m. to 7 p.m.    |
   | Friday    | 9 a.m. to 5 p.m.    |
   | Saturday  | 9.30 a.m. to 5 p.m. |

You can visit the FRC in person without an appointment
during the opening times.

## Local record offices

Local record offices do not hold a great number of records
relating to the Army, and if they do they are likely to be the
records of local volunteers and militias. If you can associate
your ancestor with a local unit and find its records you will
gain a real insight into the harsh army life.

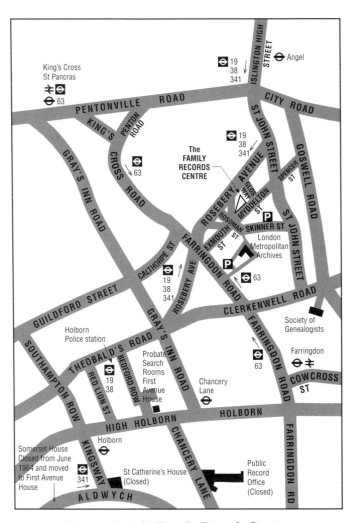

How to find the Family Records Centre

In addition local record offices may hold rolls of honour to the local war dead of the First and Second World Wars, and they usually have collections of local newspapers that you can search for army news.

You can find local record offices in the telephone directory or consult the list contained in *Record Repositories in Great Britain*. Foster and Sheppard, *British Archives*, gives a brief outline of the contents of local record offices.

# OUTLINE OF THE RECORDS AVAILABLE

The systematic keeping of army records began during the Restoration of the monarchy in the 1660s. A Secretary-at-War was appointed and it is from this point that the existence of a regular army is usually dated. There are some army records from before this date, but the main body of surviving material dates from the 18th century onwards.

During the late 17th century, the Scottish and Irish Armies were separate organisations from the English and Welsh Army, though often they effectively came under English command in times of war. The Scottish Army was only amalgamated with the English Army after the union with Scotland in 1707.

The Army, of course, took a far greater interest in the lives of its members and their families than the state does in the lives of ordinary citizens. There is therefore a huge variety of records to be found and the possibility of discovering real detail about the lives of your ancestors in the Army. Soldiers' lives were very exciting. They learned new skills in the Army and were trained for battle. They travelled around continually, and served abroad. When they went to war some won medals, some were wounded, some deserted and some were killed. Careful records were kept of all these activities and events. The Army also kept its own records of births, marriages and deaths among the families of soldiers and of other details of everyday life such as pay, promotions, and pensions. The table overleaf gives a broad outline of the range of records available.

At the Public Record Office, records are normally kept together according to the government department which created them. The vast majority of records which relate to the British Army are in the War Office or WO lettercode. Within the lettercode each collection, or class, of records is assigned a separate class number. Thus, most war diaries for the First World War are to be found in class WO 95. It is these class numbers which are referred to throughout this Pocket Guide. The table on pp. 24–7 sets out a summary of the documents held by the PRO. The following pages give more detailed information.

Records were kept for all ranks, but more of the officers' records have survived than of the lower ranks. There were

| Type of record | Availability | PRO class (where appropriate) |
|---|---|---|
| **Army births, marriages and deaths** | PRO Kew and FRC | |
| **Feudal records of 'knight service'** | | |
| Book of fees, 1198–1293 | PRO Kew | |
| Feudal aids, 1284–1431 | PRO Kew | |
| Parliamentary writs and writs of military summons | PRO Kew | |
| **Late medieval sources** | | |
| Indentures for war | PRO Kew | |
| Knight's fees | PRO Kew | |
| Agincourt Roll, 1415 | PRO Kew | E 358 |
| Chancery enrolments | PRO Kew | |
| **Tudor and Stuart musters** | | |
| Some are among papers of landed gentry | Mostly in local record offices | |
| Muster rolls | PRO Kew | |
| 'Licences to pass beyond the seas' | PRO Kew | E 157 |

| Type of record | Availability | PRO class (where appropriate) |
|---|---|---|
| **Civil War** | | |
| Names are mostly dispersed among the State Papers and records of parliamentary business | PRO Kew | |
| Certificates for the sale of crown lands | PRO Kew | E 121 |
| Muster rolls for the Scots Army in England in 1646 | PRO Kew | SP 41 |
| **Commissioned officers** | | |
| *Army Lists* since 1702 | PRO Kew, large reference libraries | WO 64–6 |
| Transfers of commissions | PRO Kew, regimental archives | |
| Records of service | PRO Kew | WO 25 |
| War Office records | PRO Kew, regimental archives | WO 76 |
| Regimental records | PRO Kew, regimental archives | |
| Pensions | PRO Kew, regimental archives | |
| Training | Royal Military College, Sandhurst | |

| Type of record | Availability | PRO class (where appropriate) |
|---|---|---|
| **Other ranks** | | |
| Soldiers' documents | PRO Kew | WO 97 |
| Pay lists and muster rolls | PRO Kew | WO 10–16 |
| Description books | PRO Kew | WO 25, WO 67 |
| Deserters | PRO Kew | E 182, WO 25 |
| Pensions | PRO Kew | |
| **Royal Artillery and Royal Engineers** (Records separate from other regiments) | PRO Kew | |
| **Militias and volunteers** | PRO Kew, local record offices | |
| **War dead and casualty returns** (by regiment and by campaign) | PRO Kew | WO 25, WO 32, WO 108 |
| **Medals and awards** (for gallantry or distinguished service, or to commemorate specific campaigns and battles) | PRO Kew, LDS Family History Centres | |
| **Courts martial** | PRO Kew | |

| Type of record | Availability | PRO class (where appropriate) |
|---|---|---|
| **First World War** | PRO Kew | |
| **Colonial regiments** | | |
| India (Indian and British Army) | PRO Kew | |
| North America | PRO Kew | |
| South Africa | PRO Kew | |
| **Ancillary services** | | |
| Barrackmasters | PRO Kew | WO 54 |
| Chaplains | PRO Kew | WO 25, WO 7 |
| Civilians | PRO Kew | WO 23, WO 25 |
| Invalids | PRO Kew | WO 25, WO 121 |
| Veterans | PRO Kew | WO 97, WO 23 |
| Medical staff | PRO Kew | WO 25, WO 54 |
| Nurses | PRO Kew | WO 25, WO 145 |
| Ordnance | PRO Kew | WO 54, WO 111 |
| Intelligence | PRO Kew | WO 37, KV 1 |
| **Prisoners of war** | PRO Kew | |

also records kept of women who worked in the armed services. First World War women's service records are in PRO class WO 398, with records of army nurses expected in early 2000. The First and Second World Wars were the only wars to embrace the population as a whole, with ordinary life being taken over by the war effort. There can be few people old enough to search the records today who will not find a parent, uncle, grandparent or great-grandparent involved in the Army during one of the world wars.

---

### ⓘ Remember

Finding out more about the military history of the time when your ancestor was in the Army will help you find your way through the mass of records available.

---

When you are researching army records just as in any of the other branches of genealogy, you will want to know their context. There are numerous books to help you with this, some of which are listed in the Further Reading section (pp. 63–4). The organisation of the Army has always been in flux and it is interesting to trace the origin and development of your ancestor's regiment. There are also numerous campaigns and battles that your ancestor might have fought in, sometimes in quite obscure places. By Victorian times the activities of the British Army spanned the globe.

The remaining sections in this Pocket Guide will explain the types of records in the order given in the table on pp. 24–7. They will explain what information you can hope to find in each type of record, what you need to know in order to start your search, and give some indication of your chances of finding an ancestor in them. They will also give suggestions for further research.

# ARMY RECORDS OF BIRTHS, MARRIAGES AND DEATHS

Regiments kept their own records of births, marriages and deaths, which give detail comparable to the information found in civil registers. The army records date from much earlier, 1761 (though they are incomplete), and were continued as independent records until 1965. Some of the registers have remained in the hands of individual regiments, but some have been collected by the General Register Office of England and Wales and can be searched at the FRC and the PRO in London (see pp. 17–20).

The relevant records and indexes at the FRC and the PRO include:

- registers of army births and marriages, 1761–1965
- registers of army deaths, 1796–1965

- indexes to births

- a list of marriage registers by regiment

- army chaplains' records of births, baptisms, marriages, deaths and burials abroad, 1796–1880, with indexes

- separate army registers for births, marriages and deaths on the Ionian Islands, 1818–64, with indexes

This makes a good starting place for a search if you do not know which regiment your ancestor was in. If his military service began after 1837, you can look him up first in the civil registration indexes also held at the FRC (see the Pocket Guide *Getting Started in Family History*), and order copies of certificates. A marriage certificate may tell you the name of the regiment or at least give you, in the husband's address, a clue to where he was stationed. Birth certificates of any children may also be informative, and even a death certificate could mention the regiment.

If you have pinpointed where a soldier was stationed at a particular time, you may find his regiment by looking up which regiments were stationed there at that time in the monthly returns. You can then search the muster books for each regiment until you find your ancestor's name. For this you will need to go to Kew.

A small number of these regimental registers are held only by the PRO at Kew, so it is worth checking there if you cannot find the register you need at the FRC.

While you are at the FRC it is also worth looking up your ancestor in the census. For this you would have to have an idea of the county where he might have been on any census night. Alternatively you can try looking him up in the name index of the 1881 census. Even after he had left the Army, a census return might give you a clue to his regiment by a reference to his pension or by indicating where his children were born. See the Pocket Guide *Using Census Returns*.

# RECORDS BEFORE 1660

Records of individuals in the Army are scant before the 1660s because there was no centralised army organisation to collect them. The affairs of the armies were bound up closely with those of the crown and the government so any records of individuals will be found amongst the records of the government business of the day.

## Feudal and medieval records

The main early sources are various records of 'indentures' or contracts made between the monarch and individual local lords for raising troops and of different payments for military service. These sources can be found scattered amongst the surviving records of the period.

## Tudors and Stuarts

In Tudor and Stuart times muster rolls were compiled by the local gentry in each county listing all those in the area who were obliged under the law to perform military service. These lists were not usually returned to central government until the 1540s, so many of them have come into the possession of local record offices. Others are held at the PRO. You can find where the roll for the area you are interested in is located in Gibson and Dell *Tudor and Stuart Muster Rolls – A Directory of Holdings in the British Isles*.

### *More Tudor and Stuart sources*

- published state papers for the Tudor and Stuart period, as these have name indexes

- Exchequer and Audit accounts for payments of wages

- 'licences to pass beyond the seas' (oaths of allegiance taken by sailors travelling overseas)

## Civil War

A good starting point for researching the period around the Civil War (1642–9) is Peacock, *Army Lists of the Roundheads and Cavaliers*, which lists officers by regiment.

Other sources for royalist soldiers include records of fines of royalists by the parliamentarians, and of some commissions on the royalist side issued by Charles I and Prince Rupert. After the Restoration of Charles II, there are records of payment and rewards given to loyal supporters.

Records of individual parliamentarians are scattered throughout the records of the period. Some good places to look include:

- certificates for the sale of crown lands (through which parliamentarians who were owed money were repaid)

- Commonwealth and Exchequer papers and other accounts

- muster rolls for the Scots Army in England in 1646

# COMMISSIONED OFFICERS

## Army Lists

The official lists of army officers known as *Army Lists* were begun in 1702 and published officially from 1740. Before then the best sources of information about officers are *English Army and Commission Registers, 1661–1714, Irish Army Lists, 1661–1685* and *George I's Army, 1714–24*, all by Charles Dalton and available at the PRO at Kew.

The official *Army Lists* are arranged by regiment. There are various indexes available for them covering different periods. From 1879 the lists give the officers' names in order of seniority with their dates of birth and promotions. From 1881 details of service are included. During the Second World War the *Army Lists* were classified and those parts of them that give biographical detail are still restricted today.

In February 1839 Lieutenant General Henry Hart started his own version of the Army lists because he felt that insufficient information was given in the official version. One interesting piece of information included by Hart was whether a commission had been purchased. If it was, you can look for it in the records for buying and selling commissions listed below. *Hart's Army Lists* were issued quarterly until 1915 and are held by the PRO at Kew.

Separate lists of officers were compiled for the:

- Royal Regiment of Artillery, 1716–1914
- Royal Engineers, 1660–1898
- Medical Officers of the Army, 1660–1960
- War Office staff, 1861–1964

## Transfers of commissions

Through the records of the transfer of commissions as people were appointed and promoted you can follow the career of an officer ancestor. The records of applications to buy and sell commissions are especially interesting because they contain supporting documents that give great detail about the applicants' circumstances. You may be able to find a record of a commission in a variety of places:

- Surviving original commissions, 1702–1823, are in WO 43/1059.

- Military entry books in the State Papers, 1679–1782, (cavalry and infantry officers only) are in SP 44.

- Militia commissions, 1782–1855, are in HO 51.

- Commission books, 1660–1803, are in WO 25.

- Notification books, 1704–1858, are in WO 4 and WO 25.

- Royal Artillery and Royal Engineers officers' commissions records, 1670–1855, are in WO 54.

- Commander-in-Chief's memoranda (for applications to purchase and sell commissions) are in WO 31 until 1871.

---

### ⓘ Remember
If you guess that your ancestor was wealthy, this is a good place to start your search.

---

Appointments and promotions were announced in the *London Gazette* and, from 1829, in the *United Service Journal and Naval and Military Magazine*. Additionally records books were kept by regiment, 1754–1808, and by date, 1773–1807. These records can now be found at the PRO in Kew (WO 25).

## Records of service

There are two types of service records: regimental records and War Office records. Regimental records start around 1755, though records do not survive for all regiments. Different regiments collected different information covering details of commissions and service and varying degrees of more personal information. There is a card index to these records at the PRO at Kew, and it is also worth investigating published regimental histories, which often give greater detail about the service records of officers.

The War Office records were begun in 1809, and appear in the records in five series covering:

- 1809–10
- 1828
- 1829
- 1847
- 1870–72

The early records were made by the officers themselves and appear in alphabetical order. Later records were arranged by regiment or year and included more detailed information.

From 1870 a new system of record keeping was introduced under the control of the Military Secretary. Standard forms were completed annually for each officer and they were bound into Army Books 83. Unfortunately enemy bombing in the Second World War destroyed the records of those officers who completed their service after 1914, though the correspondence files associated with them have survived and continue up until 1922.

You can find out more about First World War service records in S. Fowler *et al., Army Service Records of the First World War*. For records of service after 1922, you must apply to the Ministry of Defence at the address given on p. 12.

## Pensions

There were no pensions for retiring officers until 1871. Instead many officers of retirement age or who were otherwise unfit were taken off active service and put on half pay. Their names would normally still appear in the *Army Lists* and there were also separate records kept of half pay. These are not usually particularly useful to family historians, though the payment ledgers might reveal an address. Alternatively an officer might sell his commission and live on the proceeds.

From 1812 pensions were available to wounded officers. The PRO at Kew holds the registers of these, 1812–92, together with the surviving associated correspondence.

From 1708 pensions became available to the widows of officers killed on active service and in 1818 Colonel John Drouly set up a separate fund for payment of widows in need. The surviving records of widows' pensions include lists of widows, payment ledgers and correspondence relating to claims.

Provision for other dependants in need was made in 1720 through the Compassionate Fund and the Royal Bounty. In order to receive payment, dependants had to prove in an affidavit both their poverty and their relationship to an officer killed on active service. About 2000 of these affidavits are held at the PRO at Kew, arranged alphabetically, and there are also registers, ledgers and correspondence relating to these cases.

To claim these allowances it was necessary to prove relationship through baptism or birth and marriage certificates and also to produce a certificate of the officer's death. This led to a large collection of certificates accumulating among the War Office records. Many of these can be found in PRO classes WO 32 and WO 42.

## Training

There were two training colleges for officers. The Royal Military Academy was set up in Woolwich in 1741 for the artillery and engineers. The Royal Military College was set up in 1799 for the infantry and cavalry. The two were merged in 1947 to form the Royal Military College, Sandhurst. Their records include entrance applications (some complete with baptism certificates) and registers. They are kept at Sandhurst, where you can make an appointment to do research.

# OTHER RANKS

## Soldiers' documents

The records entitled Royal Hospital Chelsea soldiers' documents, 1760–1913, are the discharge papers given to men who received a pension. They can be found in the PRO class WO 97. From 1883 onwards the Royal Hospital Chelsea records also include those men who did not receive a pension. Apart from those from the early years they give an account of each soldier's career including his place of birth, age, date and occupation when he joined up, promotions, decorations or discipline received, and when and why he was discharged. They also include a description of his physical appearance to prevent others using them fraudulently. From 1883 they also give details about soldiers' families.

These soldiers' documents are the best place to start your search if you know which regiment your ancestor was in. They are arranged by regiment until 1873, when they were still divided by cavalry, infantry, artillery or corps. Luckily there is a database at the PRO at Kew, which covers the period 1760 to 1854. From 1883 the documents are arranged alphabetically by name for the whole Army together.

There is also a series of discharge documents of pensioners from the Royal Hospital Chelsea, which complement the soldiers' documents and do not duplicate them. These can be found in the PRO class WO 121.

If your ancestor was Irish, his discharge papers could have been handled by the Royal Hospital Kilmainham. These are held in a separate class, WO 119, at the PRO at Kew. The papers cover 1783 to 1822, when the Royal Hospital Chelsea took over all pensions. There are also separate records for soldiers discharged in the colonies of India, South Africa and Canada, 1772–1899. These can be found in the PRO classes WO 120, WO 69 and WO 70.

## Pay lists and muster rolls

Taken together, the pay lists and muster rolls give a very full account of a soldier's life. The pay lists follow the soldier from the date of his enlistment, through all his postings and promotions, to his death or final discharge. The muster rolls give monthly accounts (gathered into quarters) of the complete regiment giving its location and a full list of men and officers, including their dates of enlistment, rank, pay, punishments, absences, death or discharge dates. You may also find a soldier's age and trade when he enlisted and his place of birth, which were recorded for soldiers who died or were discharged. Between around 1868 and 1883 many musters also included a marriage roll giving details of soldiers' families.

The muster books and pay lists are arranged by regiment and bound in volumes covering twelve months each.

## Description books

Description books were begun in 1825 after an investigation revealed a growth in the number of fraudulent claims to have done military service. Each regiment had to record the physical appearance and service details of every man currently serving in it, which included men who had begun their service in the late 18th century and those who had their careers before them. Some details are arranged in alphabetical order by surname, and others by date of enlistment in the Army. The number of names actually collected by most regiments is small, which suggests that the records are far from complete. They can be found in the PRO class WO 25.

A second series of description books, known as the depot rolls, lists the same information for new recruits recorded as they assembled at the regimental depot. These records are more comprehensive, although they omit soldiers who enlisted where the regiment was stationed and those who transferred into one regiment from another. The PRO class for these documents is WO 67.

## Deserters

Pay was poor and conditions were hard for ordinary soldiers, so there were more deserters than you might imagine. Rewards were offered for turning them in and the bounty certificates from these have survived. There is a partial index to them at the PRO at Kew, covering rewards paid out in London and Middlesex, Bedfordshire, Berkshire, Buckinghamshire, Cambridgeshire and Cheshire. Deserters were also mentioned in casualty returns and there are also some registers of deserters.

Another place to look is in local and police newspapers of the mid-19th century, where details of deserters were advertised to encourage people to turn them in.

# Pensions

For ordinary soldiers and non-commissioned officers, pensions began in 1686. They were funded by a tax on the sale of commissions and by a levy of one day's pay per year from every soldier. Soldiers of good character were eligible to apply for pensions if they became disabled or wounded or had served for at least 20 years.

The Royal Hospital Chelsea (and the Royal Hospital Kilmainham for soldiers on the Irish Establishment from 1679 to 1822) administer most pensions. Some pensioners lived in the hospital itself but others, known as out-pensioners, were non-resident.

---

ⓘ **Remember**
The main records produced by the administration of pensions were the soldiers' documents described on pp. 39–40.

---

Records relating to out-pensions include:

- **Admission books** (WO 116, WO 117, WO 118). These are arranged in the order in which the applications were made, so you need to have an idea of the date when the soldier you are looking for was discharged.

- **Regimental registers** (WO 120, WO 23). Each regiment kept a chronological list of discharges to pension.

These give a record of service, age, birthplace, physical description, date of entry into the Army and a reason for discharge. There are partial indexes to these records.

- **Pension returns** (WO 22). The returns made by the staff officers of pensions who were responsible for making payments to out-pensioners have survived for 1842 to 1883. They are arranged by district of payment.

Records relating to in-pensioners include:

- muster rolls of the Royal Hospital Chelsea, 1702–89, 1864–5
- a list of in-pensioners, 1794–1816
- an alphabetical register, 1837–72
- admission books, 1778–96 and 1824–1917
- index of pensioners admitted 1858–1933

## ROYAL ARTILLERY AND ROYAL ENGINEERS

Most of the records discussed in this Pocket Guide originated with the War Office. Until 1855 the Royal Artillery, the Royal Engineers and the Royal Corps of Sappers and Miners were under the control of the Ordnance Office, so their records were kept separately. The records of the Royal Corps of Sappers and Miners are largely kept among those of the Royal Engineers as they were amalgamated in 1856.

Full details of the records available can be found in Fowler and Spencer, *Army Records for Family Historians*. They include officers' records of service, lists of officers, pay lists, commission books, records of commissions, pension and half pay records. For other ranks there are soldiers' documents, muster rolls, entry books of discharges, transfers and casualties, casualty records, description books and pension records.

## MILITIAS AND VOLUNTEERS

The Militia Act 1757 revived the Tudor and Stuart practice of engaging and training part-time soldiers. Militias were raised locally in counties and were mobilised in time of war by royal proclamation. As well as the militias there were the Yeomanry (cavalry) and Volunteers (local defence). These volunteer forces were called into existence at various times as needed throughout the 19th century, and in 1908 formed the bases of the Special Reserve and Volunteers and the Territorial Force, which in turn became the Supplementary Reserve and the famous Home Guard.

The records of the volunteer armies are similar in type to those found for the rest of the Army, and many can be searched among the War Office records at the PRO. For details of these see Spencer, *Records of the Militia and Volunteer Forces, 1757–1945*.

For individual units the best source of information is often the private papers of the Lords Lieutenant, who were authorised to raise them. These can often be found in local record offices. For more information on the holdings of local record offices see Gibson and Medlycott, *Militia Lists and Musters, 1757–1876*.

# WAR DEAD AND CASUALTY RETURNS

## War dead

It was customary for each regiment to keep separate rolls of the names of the dead for each major campaign. Rolls for the major campaigns of the Victorian era can be found in the PRO record classes WO 25 and WO 32. Some of these have been published and can be consulted at the PRO in Kew and at military libraries.

Under civil registration, which began in 1837, the Army kept its own regimental registers of births, marriages and deaths. Those registers kept before 1881 are held by the General Register Office of England and Wales. After 1881 the registers were returned to their relevant General

Register Office whether in England and Wales, Scotland or Ireland. The indexes to these registers can be searched in the FRC, in just the same way as other civil registration indexes (see the Pocket Guide *Using Birth, Marriage and Death Records*), and copies of certificates can be ordered. For more information, see pp. 29–30.

## War dead of the First World War

If your ancestor died or went missing presumed dead in the First World War a useful organisation to contact is the Commonwealth War Graves Commission. This is the organisation that maintains the graves all over the world of men who died in action fighting for the British and Commonwealth forces. The Commission has compiled a database of graves, and may be able to tell you where your ancestor is buried, and also his regiment and number.

▼ Commonwealth War Graves Commission
 2 Marlow Road
 Maidenhead
 Berkshire SL6 7DX
 Telephone: 01628 634221
 Internet: http://www.cwgc.org/

First World War dead are listed in *Soldiers Died in the Great War* or *Officers Died in the Great War*. These are

available on CD-ROM and microfilm. (To use the microfilm version you will need to know the regiment; for the
CD-ROM, knowing it is helpful but not essential.) The
information they give for each soldier includes: place of
birth, place of enlistment, whether he died in action or of
wounds (if known), theatre of war where death occurred,
date of death and any medals for gallantry.

---

**ⓘ Remember**

If you have no clue other than a common surname, it
may take you a long time to find your ancestor in the
lists of First World War dead.

---

## War dead of the Second World War

The Commonwealth War Graves Commission (address
on p. 47) also records the war dead and missing in the
Second World War. In addition the PRO holds registers of
war deaths in the Far East, 1941–5 (RG 33) and a roll of
honour for men and women who died during the war
(WO 304).

Records of service in the Second World War can only be
obtained by the next of kin as explained on p. 12.

## Casualty returns

The army casualty records include other reasons apart from death and wounding for absence from the regiment. They also include such reasons as desertion, discharges and authorised absences. They give details of the soldier, a brief account of the casualty and a note of the next of kin. Sometimes more personal detail is included, such as a will or a list of possessions.

---

ⓘ **Remember**
If you know a soldier's regiment but can't find any record of his discharge, the casualty returns are the next place to look.

---

The surviving returns were recorded by regiment either monthly or quarterly and include both officers and ordinary soldiers. They cover the period between 1809 and 1910 and many have been indexed. A separate series covers 1842–72.

Casualty records in the form of entry books were also kept by the Muster Master General's Office, 1797–1817. These books are in alphabetical order and give less information about each casualty.

The registers relating to payments made to the next of kin are another useful source of information on casualties.

These are arranged in alphabetical order so you do not need to know which regiment your ancestor was in. There is also a variety of registers of casualties' effects covering 1830–44, and 1862–81.

## MEDALS AND AWARDS

If you have only the name of a medal a soldier ancestor was awarded or a battle he fought in you will need to do some research in reference books to find out more about it. Medals were given for bravery, for service during a particular campaign, for length of service or to commemorate a special event.

Campaign medals were not issued much before Waterloo, but after the Waterloo campaign separate medals were issued for major battles within campaigns as well as the campaigns themselves. A full list can be found in Joslin, Litherland and Simpkin, *British Battles and Medals*. In order to distribute campaign medals, rolls had to be drawn up of all who took part. Up to the First World War these are held in one class (WO 100) in the PRO. Microfilm copies have been made and can be viewed both at the PRO and by appointment at the Family History Centres of the Church of Jesus Christ of Latter-day Saints. For more information on Family History Centres see the Pocket Guide *Getting Started in Family History*.

The table on pp. 52–3 gives the names of some of the most common and famous medals and the PRO reference to the records administering the award of each. The campaign medals of the First World War are too numerous to mention individually here. For a full guide see Fowler *et al.*, *Army Service Records of the First World War*. Campaign medal rolls compiled since 1920 are held by:

▼ Army Medal Office
  Government Buildings
  Worcester Road
  Droitwich
  Worcestershire WR9 8AU

Awards made for gallantry or meritorious service in the Second World War include the CBE, OBE, MBE, BEM, VC, DSO, MC, DCM, MM, RRC, IDM, IDSM and the BGM. The records for these are held in the PRO class WO 373.

## COURTS MARTIAL

The records of the trials of officers, 1688–1850, can be found in the PRO class WO 71 arranged in chronological order. Unfortunately similar records for 1850 to 1914 were destroyed as a result of bombing during the Second World War. The surviving records include the trial proceedings.

| Medal | Date instituted | PRO reference |
|---|---|---|
| **Gallantry and meritorious service** | | |
| Most Honourable Order of the Bath | 1725 | WO 103 |
| Meritorious Service Medal | 1846 | WO 101, WO 23 |
| Distinguished Conduct Medal | 1854 | WO 146, WO 32, WO 391 |
| Victoria Cross | 1856 | WO 32, WO 98, CAB 106 |
| Distinguished Service Order | 1886 | WO 32, WO 108, WO 389, WO 390 |
| **Campaigns** | | |
| Waterloo Medal | 1816 | WO 100, MINT 16 |
| Military General Service Medal | 1847 | WO 100 |
| New Zealand | 1861, 1863 | WO 32, WO 100 |
| South Africa | 1878 | WO 32, WO 100 |

| Medal | Date instituted | PRO reference |
|---|---|---|
| **Campaigns** | | |
| Sudan | 1884, 1896 | WO 32, WO 100 |
| Rhodesia | 1898 | WO 32, WO 100 |
| Sierra Leone | 1898 | WO 32, WO 100 |
| South Africa | 1899 | WO 32, WO 100, WO 108 |
| Somaliland | 1903 | WO 32, WO 100 |
| China | 1914 | WO 32, WO 100 |
| First World War campaign medals | 1914–18 | WO 329 |
| Kurdistan | 1925 | WO 32 |
| Nubia, Sudan | 1926 | WO 32 |
| | | |
| **Long service** | | |
| Long Service and Good Conduct Medal (for 18 years' service) | 1833 | WO 102 |

There were three possible types of courts martial of ordinary soldiers:

- general regimental (WO 89)
- district (WO 86)
- general (WO 93)

---

(i) **Remember**

Only the summaries of courts martial that have taken place within the last 75 years are available to the public.

---

# FIRST WORLD WAR RECORDS

The records of the First World War are too numerous to be discussed in any detail, but the following outline should give you an indication of where to start in your search for your relative. Records of the war dead from the First World War are explained on pp. 47–8. For a comprehensive outline of the records see Fowler *et al.*, *Army Service Records of the First World War*.

The service records of those soldiers who survived to be discharged after 1913 are held at the PRO in two separate classes, which have been or are in the process of being microfilmed:

- WO 364 (the 'unburnt documents') contains records of many of those who were discharged for medical reasons

- WO 363 (the 'burnt documents') contains many records of those who survived the war, plus those killed in action, those who died of their wounds and those who were executed. Many of these documents were burnt completely or partially as a result of enemy bombing during the Second World War, so those that survive are too fragile to be studied by the general public. Micro-filming of these documents is in progress – eventually there will be more than 20,000 reels. If your ancestor's records have not yet been filmed you can apply for them to the Ministry of Defence at the address given on p. 12.

The PRO also holds a large collection of pension records including:

- pension registers for war disabled, and for payments made to dependants of the dead and missing (PMG 9, PMG 42, PMG 11, PMG 44–47)

- pension case files (PIN 26)

## COLONIAL REGIMENTS

As colonies were gradually established in far-off con-tinents around the world during the 18th and 19th centuries, separate colonial regiments were raised when they were needed. An overall view of the colonial regiments is given in Perkins, *Regiments and Corps of the British Empire and Commonwealth: a Critical Bibliography*. Many other records are held in the national archives of the different former colonies.

The following records of men who served in colonial regiments are held at the PRO:

- soldiers' documents, 1760–1872 (WO 97)

- muster books (WO 12)

- records of colonial militia (WO 13)

- half pay returns for officers from the Canadian forces, 1783–1813 (WO 24)

- returns of ordinary soldiers and non-commissioned officers, 1806 (WO 25)

- pension records including: admission books for pensions, 1817–75 (WO 23) and 1880–1903 (WO 23); registers (WO 22)

- casualty lists and associated indexes, 1798–1817 (WO 25)

Individual colonial regiments represented in the War Office records (WO 25) at the PRO include:

- Cape Mounted Rifles
- Ceylon Rifles

- Royal Canadian Rifles
- West India Rangers

---

ⓘ **Remember**

Some regiments are mentioned in the Colonial Office records for individual colonies at the PRO.

---

## India

Until 1859 India was governed by the East India Company, which had its own army, with separate regiments for Indians and Europeans. In 1861 the European elements of the East India Company Army became part of the British Army and the Indian element became a separate Indian Army. The records of the Indian Army and many records concerning activities of the British Army in India are mostly held at:

▼ British Library India Office Collections
96 Euston Road
London NW1 2DB
Telephone: 020 7412 7677

The records at the British Library include registers of recruits, muster rolls, casualty returns, pension records and registers of births, marriages and deaths. This makes it the best place to start your search if you are certain your ancestor served in India.

There are also many references to army activities in India to be found amongst the records at the PRO including:

- lists of officers in the European regiments, 1796–1841 (WO 25)

- records of the Army Purchase Commission, 1871 (WO 74)

- pension registers and indexes of the East India Company, 1849–76 (WO 23)

- pension registers and indexes of the Indian Army, 1849–68 (WO 23)

- list of deserters from the East India Company Army, 1844–51 (WO 25)

- war diaries from Indian Army formations serving in the First World War (WO 95) and the Second World War (WO 160–179)

---

ⓘ **Remember**
You can also check the discharge records of soldiers returning from India in the depot musters for their regiments.

---

# North America

An excellent resource for tracing the colonial regiments of North America is:

▼ The National Archives of Canada
395 Wellington Street
Ottawa K1A 0N3
Canada

In the UK the discharge papers of troops serving in North America can be searched as explained on pp. 39–40, but you will be lucky to find the detail available for other sections of the Army. There are also lists of officers serving in provincial armies during the American War of Independence (T 64).

# South Africa

The records available for those men serving in units raised in South Africa itself in the South African War (1899–1902) are:

• service records (WO 126 and WO 127)

• soldiers' documents for the Imperial Yeomanry (WO 128)

• casualties (WO 129 and WO 108)

# ANCILLARY SERVICES

There was a wide range of services to support the essential fighting role of the Army, providing:

- construction and maintenance
- welfare for the soldiers and their families
- administrative services
- food
- medical services (including nurses)
- supply of equipment
- military intelligence
- training

There are numerous records relating to these activities and references for the most useful of these are given in the table on p. 27. For more detail see Fowler and Spencer, *Army Records for Family Historians.*

# PRISONERS OF WAR

There are few surviving records of prisoners of war from before the First World War. There are a few scattered lists among the War Office records, chiefly compiled with a view to exchanging prisoners rather than to keep a systematic record. The *London Gazette* is a good source of information about prisoners taken during the South African War (Boer War), though you are more likely to find mention of an officer than an ordinary soldier.

Whilst more records have been compiled of prisoners taken during the First World War, it is still difficult to find information about individuals. One reason for this is that responsibility for the monitoring of prisoners was in the hands of the International Council of the Red Cross. The Red Cross keeps comprehensive records on prisoners of war in both world wars, but these records are not open to the general public. You can make a request for a search to be made on your behalf. The request must be in writing and an hourly search fee is charged. The address to write to is:

▼ The Director
   International Welfare Department
   British Red Cross Society
   9 Grosvenor Crescent
   London SW1X 7EJ

## First World War

The most interesting records are those of the Committee on the Treatment of British Prisoners of War. These give details of interviews that were conducted with prisoners when they returned home. WO 161 also contains a small selection of repatriation reports.

## Second World War

A list entitled *Prisoners of War* includes 169,000 prisoners from the British Empire who were ascertained to be under German control on 30 March 1945. A separate list in PRO class WO 392 covers all British and Dominions prisoners held by the Germans and Italians, 1939–45.

There are more sources for prisoners held by the Japanese including:

- an alphabetical card index of 57,000 names (WO 345)

- registers of camps in Singapore (WO 367)

- hospital records for prisoners in Asia (WO 347)

- further alphabetical lists (WO 392, FO 916, CO 980)

- records of escape and evasion (AIR 40, WO 208)

- interrogations of liberated prisoners (WO 203, WO 208)

## Korean War

There is a series of Historical Records and Reports on the Korean War in PRO class WO 308. These include lists of prisoners from the British Commonwealth. Another list can be found in WO 208 and general correspondence about prisoners is located in WO 162, WO 32 and DO 35.

# FURTHER READING

*Alphabetical Guide to certain War Office and Other Military Records preserved in the Public Record Office* (List & Indexes LIII)

J. Foster and J. Sheppard, *British Archives: A Guide to Archive Resources in the United Kingdom* 2nd ed. (London, 1988)

S. Fowler and W. Spencer, *Army Records for Family Historians* 2nd ed. (PRO, 1998)

S. Fowler, W. Spencer and S. Tamblin, *Army Service Records of the First World War* (PRO, 1998)

J. Gibson and A. Dell, *Tudor and Stuart Muster Rolls: A Directory of Holdings in the British Isles* (FFHS, 1991)

J. Gibson and M. Medlycott, *Militia Lists and Musters, 1757–1876* (FFHS, 1994)

Imperial War Museum, *Officers Died in the Great War* (London 1921–2)

Imperial War Museum, *Soldiers Died in the Great War* (London, 1921)

E. Joslin, A. Litherland, and B. Simpkin, *British Battles and Medals* (Spink, 1988)

E. Peacock, *Army Lists of the Roundheads and Cavaliers* (London, 1863)

R. Perkins, *Regiments and Corps of the British Empire and Commonwealth: a Critical Bibliography* (1994)

*Record Repositories in Great Britain* 11th ed. (PRO/Royal Commission on Historical Manuscripts, 1999)

W. Spencer, *Records of the Militia and Volunteer Forces, 1757–1945* (PRO, 1997)

A. Taylor, *Discovering Military Uniforms* (Shire Publications)

R. J. Wilkinson-Latham, *Discovering British Military Badges and Buttons* (Shire Publications, 1972)

T. Wise and S. Wise, *A Guide to Military Museums and Other Places of Military Interest* 9th ed. (Doncaster, 1999)